W9-CBC-500

Praise for
Plastic Donuts

"Jeff Anderson's insightful book gives us a fresh perspective on what it means to please God through our giving. Read it to gain refreshment for your soul and a challenge to grow more generous."

—CHUCK BENTLEY, CEO of Crown
   Financial Ministries

"This is a fresh and worthy call to kingdom building through a life marked by generosity. The *Plastic Donuts* message is desperately needed in our lives and churches today."

—GORDON MACDONALD, chancellor
   of Denver Seminary

"The Plastic Donut illustration helped me focus for the first time on my Father's reaction to my giving. This understanding is transformational."

—HOWARD DAYTON, founder and CEO
   of Compass–finances God's way

"Jeff Anderson walks the walk of surrendered stewardship."

> —RON BLUE, founding director
> of Kingdom Advisors

"Our gifts to God matter. He desires that we give because of what he wants *for* us, not *from* us. I challenged my congregation to read this outstanding book."

> —RANDY POPE, pastor of Perimeter Church,
> Duluth, Georgia

"*Plastic Donuts* is a paradigm-shifting powerhouse."

> —PATRICK JOHNSON, chief architect
> of GenerousChurch

"An investment of two hours can forever change the way you think, teach, and practice giving. *Plastic Donuts* will bring you to the heart of God and show you a new way to enjoy Him forever."

> —DR. ROGER PATTERSON, senior pastor of West
> University Baptist and Crosspoint Church,
> Houston, Texas

"*Plastic Donuts* is a fresh approach to living and giving. The concepts help readers move beyond legalism to see God as a loving Father who desires to bless His children."

> —MICKEY RAPIER, directional leader at Fellowship
> Bible Church Northwest Arkansas, Rogers,
> Arkansas

"Jeff Anderson provides a fresh, biblical look at giving. I found myself eagerly turning the next page to discover what God had for me to consider personally."

> —TODD HARPER, president of Generous Giving

PLASTIC
DONUTS

GIVING THAT DELIGHTS
THE HEART OF THE FATHER

PLASTIC
DONUTS

JEFF ANDERSON

MULTNOMAH
BOOKS

PLASTIC DONUTS

All Scripture quotations, unless otherwise indicated, are taken from the Holy Bible, New International Version®, NIV®. Copyright © 1973, 1978, 1984, 2011 by Biblica Inc.™ Used by permission of Zondervan. All rights reserved worldwide. www.zondervan.com. Scripture quotations marked (AMP) are taken from The Amplified Bible. Copyright © 1954, 1958, 1962, 1964, 1965, 1987 by The Lockman Foundation. Used by permission. Scripture quotations marked (ESV) are taken from The Holy Bible, English Standard Version, copyright © 2001 by Crossway Bibles, a division of Good News Publishers. Used by permission. All rights reserved. Scripture quotations marked (NASB) are taken from the New American Standard Bible®. © Copyright The Lockman Foundation 1960, 1962, 1963, 1968, 1971, 1972, 1973, 1975, 1977, 1995. Used by permission. (www.Lockman.org). Scripture quotations marked (NKJV) are taken from the New King James Version®. Copyright © 1982 by Thomas Nelson Inc. Used by permission. All rights reserved. Scripture quotations marked (NLT) are taken from the Holy Bible, New Living Translation, copyright © 1996, 2004, 2007. Used by permission of Tyndale House Publishers Inc., Carol Stream, Illinois 60188. All rights reserved.

Italics in Scripture quotations reflect the author's added emphasis.

Some anecdotes and stories have been changed to protect the identities of the persons involved.

Hardcover ISBN 978-1-60142-528-7
eBook ISBN 978-1-60142-529-4

Copyright © 2012, 2013 by Jeff Anderson
Previously published by Acceptable Gift Inc. in 2012.

Cover design and photo by Faceout Studio, Charles Brock

Published in the United States by Multnomah, an imprint of the Crown Publishing Group, a division of Penguin Random House LLC, New York.

MULTNOMAH® and its mountain colophon are registered trademarks of Penguin Random House LLC.

Library of Congress Cataloging-in-Publication Data
Anderson, Jeff, 1970 February 5–
    Plastic donuts : giving that delights the heart of the Father / Jeff Anderson. — First edition.
      pages cm
    ISBN 978-1-60142-528-7 — ISBN 978-1-60142-529-4 (electronic)
  1. Generosity—Religious aspects—Christianity. 2. Wealth—Religious aspects—Christianity.
3. Christian giving. 4. Christian stewardship. 5. Finance, Personal—Religious aspects—
Christianity. I. Title.
    BV4647.G45A53 2013
    248'.6—dc23   2013009002

Printed in the United States of America
2020

20 19 18 17 16 15 14

SPECIAL SALES
For information, please e-mail specialmarketscms@penguinrandomhouse.com or call
1-800-603-7051.

To Autumn Joy.
You are God's special gift to your
mother and me, and the one God
would use to teach me about the
Father's perspective.

I am amply supplied, now that I have received from Epaphroditus the gifts you sent. They are a fragrant offering, an acceptable sacrifice, pleasing to God.

—Apostle Paul, Philippians 4:18

Contents

Introduction

Plastic Donuts. They're everywhere, but few things are more misunderstood. When they do come up in conversation, it feels awkward, even confusing. It's like something's missing.

Did you know the first murder in recorded history followed some hard feelings between two brothers over Plastic Donuts? That could explain why we hear so many dos and don'ts centered on the subject. The problem is, the rules contradict one another. That's a real tragedy for all of us, because these simple Donuts can bring such joy and delight to the heart of God.

They show up in the stories of some of the biggest

events in history. A man named Noah gave them after being stranded on an ark. God responded with a rainbow in the sky.

Another man, named Solomon, gave some Donuts, and God visited him in a dream.

A fellow named Cornelius gave them and received a visit from an angel.

Make no mistake. This is important stuff.

I'm Jeff Anderson, and I'll start by sharing a story about a Plastic Donut that was given to me. It was a gift that changed me forever.

For years I had been trying to understand more about giving, and more about God. I had wrestled with the issues, debated, stayed up late to study, even lost sleep. I was given a Plastic Donut just in time, and it opened my eyes to giving from God's perspective.

If you'll stick with me (it's a short book, right?), I trust you'll enjoy the experience. I hope you will learn new things about God. And I hope you will look deeply into yourself—where you will be reminded of the power of a Father's love and the power of your gifts.

With all the different messages spelling out the

rules of giving, wouldn't it be great to finally get some clarity and peace about this issue? I'll make you a promise. When you start to see giving from God's perspective, the lights will come on. You'll see that you really can feel good about your gifts.

And it gets back to a Plastic Donut. A simple, easily dismissed token of love holds the secret to getting your mind and your heart on the same page. Isn't that what you've been looking for?

RELAX

I'm not a professional fund-raiser, and this isn't a book about pressure or guilt. Rather it's a message about the power of gifts, the way we give, and who we give to.

The Plastic Donut can open your eyes to God in a way that clears up questions and dispels anxiety. What you'll experience brings enormous freedom. You'll feel the weight of uncertainty being lifted from your shoulders, and you'll be challenged by what you learn about your gifts.

Some of the ways we've been encouraged to give are

weak, but some of the ways we've convinced ourselves *not* to give are also questionable. Fair enough?

I was in my twenties when I first heard teachings about money in church. I recall hearing that we should spend less than we earn, avoid debt, and give 10 percent to the church. But there was a problem.

I had lived out these principles since childhood. My parents taught me about tithing. I enjoyed calculating my tithe because I enjoyed counting my money. And I learned to manage my spending and avoid debt mainly because I craved cash more than stuff. I was doing the "right" things. Still, something was missing. I had a growing sense of financial peace, but spiritual peace about giving was lacking.

Was there more to pleasing God with my money than having a budget and a clean tithing record? This question sparked a hunger in me to understand how God views giving and how my giving could actually get His attention.

We've all heard sermons and read statistics about the meager rate of giving, even among churchgoers. Yes, greed and materialism are real forces in our lives. But don't you think that, deep down inside, Christians have a desire to give?

Still, the mixed messages we hear on the subject can be frustrating. The appeals, demands, and "answers" will continue to bombard us. There must be a better way.

That's where the Plastic Donut comes in.

ONE

The Plastic Donut

Autumn Joy toddled across the room and stood at the edge of my laptop-centered view. I was in task mode, typing away while sitting in the living-room recliner. With Shirley Temple curls bouncing around her face, my eighteen-month-old daughter looked up at me. I looked at her. Then she handed me a Plastic Donut from her kitchen play set.

I looked at the Donut and back at my daughter. She stood waiting for a response. So I put the Donut up to my mouth and said with great animation, "Yummm, yummm... Thank you, Autumn! This is *soooo goood.*"

Then something beautiful happened. Her big brown eyes widened, and her lips pushed a giant smile against her puffy cheeks. She stood up on her toes, shrugged her shoulders up to her ears, and let out a high-pitched squeal.

After soaking in the experience for a few seconds, she ran back to her kitchen and brought me a little pink spoon. Again I responded, showing her my pleasure and approval. The cycle continued a few more times as I collected plastic pieces from her kitchen set.

For Autumn, this exercise in giving gifts kept bringing her back to Daddy. For me, it kept me looking for my child to return to my side. I was moved by the exchange. I loved the interaction and connection. I was so pleased.

The whole experience wasn't about the Donut (and believe me, I like donuts). If one of Autumn's older brothers had brought me a Plastic Donut, it wouldn't have been the same. Somehow this gift was exactly right coming from my daughter, even if it was just a toy.

THE AHA MOMENT

I didn't see it coming, but at that moment it occurred to me: this is how our giving must feel from God's perspective. Our gifts to Him are like Plastic Donuts. God does not need our gifts or our money. But like a child's gift that moves her father, our gifts can really get God's attention.

For my daughter, the feedback from our interaction inspired continued giving. If I had not paid attention to her or had withheld my delight, she would have stopped.

She was learning about the power of a pleasing gift and learning about connecting with me as her father. Meanwhile, I was learning about God and how to better connect with Him as my Father.

For years I had thought a lot about the receivers of my gifts: my church, my neighbor, my chosen charities. And I had studied the benefits that come to me as a giver. But I hadn't given much thought to my gift from God's viewpoint. Could it be that God desires a similar Plastic-Donut experience when I give to Him?

And what about the thrill my daughter received when she saw the joy on my face? I had never before pictured the act of giving as something that elicits such delightful reactions. Had I been missing opportunities to connect with God in deeper ways?

Suddenly I could understand giving from a different perspective.

QUESTIONS. YES, WE HAVE QUESTIONS

We like to give and receive gifts. We have a desire to honor God and would like to understand what God's Word says about giving. The problem is, our noisy culture keeps providing more "answers" to our questions that fail to clear up the confusion.

I want to know the truth. I want some clarity and confidence in what I believe and how I live. How about you?

Here's a sampling of the questions about giving we hear most often:

- What's the "right" amount to give?
- Does the tithe still apply to modern-era people?
- Is the first 10 percent required, and everything else is a freewill offering?
- What should be our motivation in giving?

- Does it even matter what we give as long as we have good hearts?

Have you ever played a new board game when you were still unclear about the rules? It's awkward. You don't know when you're making the right moves. That's how giving feels for so many people.

There has to be some clarity in the Bible that brings us a better feeling about giving—a feeling like the deep connection my daughter and I felt when I received that Plastic Donut. Would God really have left us to our own devices to figure this thing out?

WAY TOO MANY VOICES

After spending many years far from God, a young man rediscovers his faith. He visits a large church in his city. In a message on giving, the pastor rejects the concept of tithing. He says it doesn't apply today—just like animal sacrifices and other areas of the Old Testament law. Instead, this pastor refers to something called "grace giving." The young man appreciates learning something new, and this teaching makes sense to him.

A few weeks later, he visits another church in the same city. The pastor there is starting a series on tithing. He has reached the part where he's asking for tithing commitments. This seems to make sense, but it contradicts the teaching of the other pastor. The young man leaves church that day wondering what the Bible really does say about giving.

Some leaders use New Testament teachings to prove the Old Testament no longer applies. Others find verses in the New Testament that they say prove certain Old Testament rules still apply. Some teachers encourage giving based on the prosperity they say will follow. Others caution against "robbing God"—to avoid the curses that they say would follow. And some teachers combine these two views as one, while still others reject both.

NO BASHING ALLOWED

It's fun to point out inconsistencies, but let's cut our church and ministry leaders some slack. Pastors and Bible teachers are not the only ones struggling to land on a unified, authoritative approach. Those who come with questions also tend to provide answers.

The senior-adult Sunday school class members have strong opinions about how young people *should* give. Meanwhile, the young folks have their own ideas about what giving should look like for them. Blogs and chat rooms have "answers" too. Like armchair quarterbacks breaking down Sunday's game, plenty of commentators weigh in on matters of where, why, and how much we should give.

I imagine in the midst of all this you have heard some troubling things. There are enough financial scandals on record to cast doubt on church and ministry giving. Calling out those who were responsible for misusing donated funds can make us feel better about a subject we don't fully understand. But never lose sight of this: "the church"—meaning pastors, speakers, evangelists, ministry leaders, name your favorite target—is not corrupt. Church leaders are seeking answers to questions about giving just like the rest of us. And it's their job to be as clear as they can on a very dicey subject.

It would be wrong to use the misdeeds or the manipulative tactics of a very few as an excuse to ignore our own unresolved questions about giving. Remember, we all need personal clarity from Scripture when a question arises.

SILENCE CAN BE A PROBLEM TOO

Sometimes the *lack* of talk about giving is the problem.

Put yourself in your pastor's shoes. Can you imagine standing in the pulpit and bringing up the subject of money? The best-intentioned leader (you're the pastor, remember?) would struggle with the challenge of teaching on this topic without appearing to have a conflict of interest.

The congregation expects the lights to work and the building to be clean. Just imagine wrestling with the additional needs for expanded facilities or more staff while at the same time faithfully supporting projects for missions and the poor. Is it any wonder pastors are tempted to avoid a deep discussion of the subject of money?

Churches and faith-based charities have a God-given passion for their particular causes. Bold appeals for monetary support are expected—and scriptural. Let's give pastors and ministry leaders a break and recognize that the disconnect we feel about giving could be caused by our lack of a clear, biblical perspective on the topic. How many years (okay, centuries) have we been wondering about these things?

If you've received this book from your pastor or a ministry leader, you know they want to bring light to the subject. Here's an opportunity to get on the same page and pray for all our eyes to be opened.

EXPECT GOOD THINGS

I have sought clarity on giving for decades, and I have benefitted from lessons taught from various perspectives. In my work with church and ministry leaders, I see how giving matters to their organizations. I've experienced this personally while serving on finance committees and on the elder board of my church.

I have talked about giving with the homeless at a downtown shelter. And I've discussed the topic with the affluent while dining on steak and lobster. I have talked with my grandfather about giving and have shared the same concepts with a class of fourth-grade students.

While Christians have debated these issues and reached a number of different conclusions, I am convinced that the Plastic Donut is a metaphor for giving that cuts through the noise and offers clarity. It captures an approach to giving that discards pat answers while uncovering truths that can be trusted and helpful for everyone. Even better, when your questions about giving can be answered with confidence, your connection with your heavenly Father will grow stronger.

MONEY ON MY MIND

As a kid, I cared a great deal about money. One Christmas I received a small red safe to use for storing my cash. I uncovered the safe a few years ago while helping my mom clean out her attic. I could still remember the combination: 30 on the left dial, 110 on the right!

Saving money was gratifying to me. I often wanted

to buy things, but then I would change my mind due to a stronger desire to keep the cash. I was frugal but also selfish. This sometimes comes with the territory of being a saver. Savers like to accumulate. Spenders like to release. Both have to confront their respective tendencies in order to give in ways that God designed.

As a child, I put 10 percent of my earnings in the colored envelopes at church. I never thought about giving less than that. But neither did I think about giving more. This hard-and-fast standard created a tension in my heart, one that would play out in my mind for years. When the subject of giving comes up, a similar tension may arise in you.

I went to college and majored in accounting, thinking it would be a way to keep close tabs on this thing called money. After graduating, I obtained my CPA license, but it wasn't long before I grew less interested in tracking other people's money and decided to go into business to make my own money.

Along the way, I continued to wrestle with one particular money matter: giving.

THINGS ARE LOOKING UP

As a money counter who needed to know the price of everything, I especially wanted to know the price of this spiritual practice called giving. I had questions such as, "How much should I give?" and "Is there a biblical giving standard?"

Back to that occasion when I first heard money addressed in church as a legitimate topic for discussion. I was sitting in a Sunday school class with my new bride. Later, as we walked to our car after church, she turned to me and said, "I believe someday you will be involved in a ministry like this." Neither of us knew how prophetic her words were. At the time, all I knew was that I couldn't get thoughts about giving off my mind.

After my accounting career, I enjoyed five years as a full-time stock trader. Some of my life's most powerful lessons were learned during that period. There were some dark days during my trading journey, mostly because I was accustomed to thinking like the crowd. But when I learned to think *against the crowd,* things changed for the better. When the crowd was buying, it was often time to sell. When the crowd was selling, it was often time to buy.

This against-the-grain thinking can be helpful when you are trying to understand giving. After the Plastic Donut encounter with my daughter, my views on giving changed. I saw more clearly why the joy of giving can seem so elusive. It's hard to experience it without looking up to the Father.

Often, instead of looking up with my gift, I was looking down. Instead of pondering God's reaction to my giving, I was occupied with my own feelings on the subject. Instead of giving to the One unseen, I'd been giving to what I could see.

The Donut experience gave me a fresh perspective that connected with my study of Scripture and started to make sense. Along the way I found simple truths and simple answers to my questions.

REACHING FOR THE RESET BUTTON

Let's see how feelings about giving can shift from guilt and confusion to being a foundational part of our deeper connection to God our Father. We all want our gifts to matter to God, and we might even dare to believe they can bring a smile to His face. So let's step out from the crowd and away from the noise. Let's think against the grain of the prevailing approaches. Let's reach for the reset button and discover new answers to our questions.

- How does God respond to my gifts?
- Does God really care about what I give?
- Does He like some gifts and dislike others?

I'm ready if you are. Let's find out together.

▬ ▬ ▬ ▬ ▬ ▬ Thoughts on Giving

Have you ever received a gift from a child that touched your heart?

Do you think it's possible that God takes delight in our gifts—just as an earthly father reacts to a child's simple, heartfelt gift?

TWO

What Is Acceptable?

Everyone told me having a daughter would be different. After having three sons, I figured I knew what was coming. But sure enough, it happened. My baby girl stole my heart. And years later, I'm still smitten.

It's not hard to imagine God being enamored of His children. The young sons of Adam and Eve were surely adorable in His sight. We don't know much about these brothers, Cain and Abel, but surprisingly we know about their gifts. Like my Donut experience as a father, God enjoys receiving gifts.

ABEL'S GIFT

> When it was time for the harvest, Cain presented
> some of his crops as a gift to the LORD. Abel also
> brought a gift—the best of the firstborn lambs
> from his flock. The LORD accepted Abel and his
> gift, but he did not accept Cain and his gift.
> (Genesis 4:3–5, NLT)

It was a unique time in the lives of the earth's first
sons. Sin and imperfection were relatively new, and their
destructive effect on what God had made was well un-
derway. Yet I'm sure much of what God had made was
still quite wonderful. Resources were abundant. Needs
were scarce. No one was poor, orphaned, or sick.

But there were gifts to God. On one occasion, the
brothers presented gifts from their profits. Interestingly,
God viewed the gifts differently. One gift was viewed
favorably; the other was not. The Hebrew meaning of
the original text (*sha'ah*) suggests God regarded, re-
spected, and gazed at Abel's gift in a special way.

Sibling rivalries go way back. God's response of preferring one gift and rejecting the other exposed the brothers' rivalry. Cain's feelings were hurt and he became angry. You may know the rest of this sad story. Acting on his emotions, Cain took his brother into a field, and there he killed him.

This is heavy drama to process so early in the Bible. Adam and Eve's fall and expulsion from the garden were enough to derail the feel-good beginnings of the creation account. Now the first act of murder by one son against another is a crusher. What a scandal! Yet from God's perspective, a bright spot shines through it all—Abel's gift.

Several thousand years later, a God-inspired writer travels down memory lane. Abel receives the first mention among history's faith heroes. The description that would accompany this honor states that he gave "a *more acceptable* sacrifice" to God (Hebrews 11:4, ESV).

Still today, people are curious about Cain and Abel's gifts. For a story with so few details, theologians have many ideas. This much is clear: in the very beginning, God showed great interest in the gifts from His children.

Like Plastic Donuts given to a little girl's daddy, these gifts to the heavens trigger reactions from God. But perhaps the most significant lesson is this: Not all gifts are the same to Him. Not all gifts are acceptable.

ACCEPTABLE...A PLEASING WORD

The English language doesn't have a word that fully expresses the biblical idea of *acceptable*. As we use the word, it sometimes means "barely good enough." A synonym of sorts to *adequate* or *just squeaking by*. But in God's vocabulary, *acceptable* is a powerful concept.

David understood its meaning:

> Let the words of my mouth and the meditation of my heart be *acceptable* in Your sight, O Lord, my strength and my Redeemer. (Psalm 19:14, NKJV)

Your Bible translation may use the word *acceptable,* or it may say *pleasing.* The words often are used interchangeably in the Scriptures. Isaiah spoke about the kind of fast that is *acceptable* to God (see Isaiah 58:5).

He was referring to a type of fast that pleases God—certainly not one that is "barely good enough." Paul instructed us to present our bodies as a "living sacrifice, holy, *acceptable to God*..." (Romans 12:1, NKJV). This would be a sacrifice that is pleasing to God.

When I think of *acceptable* in these ways, I imagine a word that could encapsulate the feeling I had when my daughter gave me the Plastic Donut. It's a word that expresses delightful, surprising, perfect, tearful, proud, ecstatic happiness. What word would that be? It's what *acceptable* means.

In David's song to the Lord, perhaps what he really was saying was this:

Let all that I say and all that I think about bring a big, joyful smile to Your face, and make You really proud of me.

Getting the picture?

PLEASING GOD. REALLY, IT'S OKAY

Like any child who seeks to please his Father, Jesus was no different. He said, "For I always do what pleases him"

(John 8:29). And we know God was pleased with Jesus. The Father said so, with a voice that boomed from heaven (see Matthew 17:5).

Even Moses, who enjoyed direct access to God, wanted to know that God was pleased with him (see Exodus 33:13, 16).

But when it comes to our pleasing God, bad doctrine often gets in the way. Some people view it as a performance or a way to appease God—or maybe to satisfy His demands. Of course, this is wrong.

Others react negatively to the idea of pleasing God because of their past inability to please the people who are most important to them: a parent, a spouse, a boss, a friend. This is unfortunate. We may carry baggage from ruptured relationships on earth, but our relationship with God is different. It is pure. We can please God, and for the right reasons. Our greatest aim in life should be to please Him, whether we are on earth or in heaven (see 2 Corinthians 5:9).

The thought of pleasing God should be comforting to us, and our gifts are one tool that help us please Him.

It felt good to Abel to please God with his gift, and it felt good to God to receive it.

Part of our challenge with the idea of *acceptable* is that in everyday life we see varying grades of acceptability. We see high, medium, low—or good, better, best.

But in Scripture we don't see tiers of relative merit. God does not set forth degrees of acceptability. It is either acceptable or it is not. And the acceptable standard is a very favorable one.

A PLEASING AROMA

Noah knew about God's fascination with gifts from His children. After the flood, Noah exited the ark with his family and offered some of all the clean animals and clean birds as a sacrifice to God (see Genesis 8:20). What a bonfire that must have been!

This got God's attention. He smelled "the pleasing aroma" and then made a covenant to never again destroy all living things (see Genesis 8:21). The word *nichowach* (pleasing aroma) means soothing, quieting, tranquilizing. Like steaming hot coffee on a cold day, God has His sweet aroma moments too.

Humanity's sin nature could not be reversed (see Genesis 8:21). Yet people could still give gifts that brought a favorable reaction from God. In Noah's case, a smile of vibrant colors across the sky was a reminder of the pleasing relationship God desires with His children (see Genesis 9:13). If you want to know what launched the rainbow among the clouds, think of Noah's gift.

Eight hundred years later God formalized the gift-giving practices. Under the Law of Moses, the Israelites presented "acceptable" offerings (Leviticus 1:3; 22:20). The animals used for sacrifice were to be perfect. From the heavens above, God took in the pleasing aroma (see Leviticus 1:9, 13, 17). And from the earth below, people took comfort in knowing God was touched by their gifts.

AN ACCEPTABLE LAMB

Thanks be to God for his indescribable gift!
(2 Corinthians 9:15)

Fast forward another fifteen hundred years. During a certain Passover holiday week, acceptable lambs were being offered at the temple in Jerusalem. Meanwhile, a most unique gift was being presented to God on a hillside nearby.

This gift was offered on a cross. This gift was God's very own Lamb. This gift was…Jesus.

Like the acceptable animal gifts from the past, Jesus too was "a lamb without blemish or defect" (1 Peter 1:19). And as hard as it may be for us to comprehend, this gift of the life of His Son was "a fragrant offering and sacrifice to God" (Ephesians 5:2).

Many who witnessed this indescribable gift put the pieces together. Suddenly the history of sacrifices made sense. The gifts of the past had been a picture of this perfect gift—a *completely acceptable gift.*

ACCEPTABLE GIFTS TODAY

A lot changed after Jesus gave the one indescribable gift. Animal sacrifices faded away, but acceptable gifts to God did not. God continues to find pleasure in our gifts.

The Christians living in Philippi had given gifts of money, which Paul described as "a fragrant offering, an *acceptable* sacrifice, pleasing to God" (Philippians 4:18). Another translation gives us this perspective on the gifts: "[They are the] fragrant odor of an offering and sacrifice which God welcomes and in which He delights" (AMP).

Our gifts today can do a lot of good. They can feed the hungry, heal the sick, encourage the brokenhearted, and spread the good news. But most importantly, they can please God in heaven, connecting His children to Him.

Think about that.

TRUTHS, NOT SECRETS

We are beginning to see important truths about giving from the Plastic Donut. The same truths are played out in the Scriptures. One of the most surprising to many of us is this: *our gifts can delight the heart of the Father, bringing a smile to His face. These are acceptable gifts.*

This truth is not new, but it has been hidden from many of us. As we continue exploring together, we will uncover four breakout truths. We call them the *Acceptable Gift truths*. These truths bring clarity and provide reliable answers to the most common questions about giving. And they open our eyes to the ways our gifts can bring delight to God.

▬ ▬ ▬ ▬ ▬ ▬ Thoughts on Giving

How does the Bible's use of the word *acceptable* change your thinking about giving God an acceptable gift?

What is the first thing that comes to mind when you think about pleasing God?

THREE

Does the Amount Matter?

With three young boys in our home, we are a family of jokesters and cutups. Our youngest son, Gunnar, doesn't mind being the object of family jokes, and he sure doesn't mind initiating them.

One day he came up to me with his hands behind his back and a goofy grin on his face. "Here you go, Dad," he said. He held out his hands and handed me...the Plastic Donut. Then he busted out laughing. His donut gift to me was a joke from him. I thought it was funny too. To show my approval, I wrapped him in a headlock and gave him a bare-knuckle noogie on his tightly shaved head.

After hearing me use the Donut illustration in

sermons and teachings, Gunnar figured out the Plastic Donut carried a special meaning to me. Even at age seven, he understood that a plastic toy given by a school-age boy would not produce the same effect on me as it did when given by his younger sister as a toddler. He knew that not all gifts are received the same way—even when the gifts are identical.

Many of us are playing jokes with our gifts to God. It may look like a few dollars in the plate, a small check here and there, or a sporadic string of checks that are discontinued during the summer. For some, even steady, 10 percent giving might be considered a joke in God's eyes.

You've heard it said: "Every gift is special." "Every gift can make a difference." "No gift is too small." For secular campaign fund-raising, this might be true. But when it comes to giving to God, there is a problem with these ideas. Not all gifts are special to God. And not all gifts are acceptable.

King David knew that a gift that cost him nothing was worth nothing to God. The king was seeking out a location to offer a gift of burnt offerings. An attractive altar arrangement and a team of oxen had been offered to David for free. But he wanted his giving to be the acceptable kind, so he insisted on paying for the items at full market price (see 2 Samuel 24:22–25).

This brings us to our first truth about acceptable gifts (ones that get God's attention). When it comes to our gifts, *the amount matters.*

When the gift amount matters to us, it can matter to God too. When the amount doesn't matter to us, it doesn't matter to God. The toy donut did not matter to Gunnar, so it was not an acceptable gift from him.

AMOUNTS THAT MATTER TO US

We all have amounts that matter to us. They may be home mortgage payments, rent payments, car payments, vacation packages, furniture purchases, club memberships. Because these amounts matter, we are diligent to set aside the money.

The question is, *what are the amounts that matter to you?* Do your gifts to God fit in this category? Are you as diligent in making careful provision for your gifts to God as you are in making other financial decisions?

If you have ever borrowed money to buy a home, you know banks will loan money based on their projection of what you can afford. The affordability calculations make assumptions about how people with your income level might live. The calculations likely don't take into account other amounts, such as your gifts to God. If you want to give gift amounts that matter to you, then it's up to you to leave room in your budget.

When people take advantage of the maximum amount that mortgage brokers and car financiers will loan, they commit a large portion of their incomes to these items. In effect, the amounts that matter are decided *for* them.

THE AMOUNT MATTERS TO THE HEART

John is a twenty-six-year old software engineer for a growing technology company. He's pretty satisfied with his $85,000 annual salary, and he makes maximum contributions to his 401(k).

He enjoys his $1,500-per-month apartment near the mountains and his new mini SUV. He is particularly glad he purchased the special edition sport package to accommodate his skis in the winter and bicycle in the summer months. John is also excited about beginning his new life with Amy, his soon-to-be bride.

When Amy saw the small velvet box that John pulled from a pocket, it took her breath away. But when she opened the box, her reaction changed. She tried not to appear disappointed. When she learned John had purchased the ring for just $250, she was devastated.

Amy is far from a materialistic person, yet she still found the gift to be deeply insulting. She sobbed, asking John if he really loved her.

John was embarrassed, and also felt a bit defensive. Amy's reaction to the ring stung. Then John said something he later would regret: "The amount I paid for the ring doesn't matter so much. It's the heart that counts."

In my discussions with Christians about giving, no opinion has been more frequently expressed than this one: "The amount doesn't really matter. It's all about the heart."

I understand the good intentions behind this statement. The problem is, the message is wrong. Often we pull the heart card to avoid deeper questions about the amount we give. While the heart is crucial to the act of giving and to our gifts (we'll talk about that soon), the amount matters too. In fact, it's *the amount* that helps engage the heart.

During the famous message we call the Sermon on the Mount, Jesus taught the connection between our hearts and our amounts. "For where your treasure is, there your heart will be also" (Matthew 6:21).

Wherever you invest your money, a force pulls your heart along with it. You have no choice in the matter, just like the force of gravity pulls an object toward the center of the earth. So if you spend an amount that matters very little to you, it will move your heart very little. If you spend an amount that matters more to you, it will move a more meaningful amount of your heart in that direction. The amount gets the attention of your heart.

I used to have two very different cars. One was old and the other was much newer and worth a lot more. In the evenings after work, I would take my boys outside where they would ride bikes. The driveway was a great place to turn around, but occasionally they would get their handlebars too close and bump up against the cars. If they collided with my old car, I would run over to help them up and make sure they were okay. If they collided with my new car, I would run over to make sure my *car* was okay. Then I would scold the kids for being careless.

Why the difference in my reaction? Because the new car had attracted more of my treasure, and therefore it had captured more of my heart.

LIFE AND LIFESTYLE

As a young adult, I was comfortable with giving at a level of 10 percent. (This is common after practicing tithing for many years.) When my income was rising, the 10 percent was growing too. But the other 90 percent was growing faster. And even though my 10 percent gifts were increasing in amount, the remaining 90 percent was focused completely on feeding my lifestyle. The truth is, the 10 percent wasn't moving my heart like it had in the past.

If I wanted to go on a weekend trip, I would. If I

wanted to buy a new gadget, I would. If I wanted to speculate on a stock tip, I would. Much of my time and attention were spent considering other things to do with the 90 percent. I spent very little time thinking about the 10 percent I was giving away and zero time imagining a life of giving more than that.

I was diligent in giving an amount to God and would be welcomed as a faithful tither in today's church culture. But I was not giving an amount that really mattered to me. It was not an amount that influenced my lifestyle.

What I didn't realize was that my lifestyle had frozen my giving at the 10 percent level. When it came to my finances, my lifestyle had all the influence.

The issue is not about my needing to sacrifice my lifestyle. The issue is about my giving a gift that is connected to my heart. But because I have a tendency to attach myself to my possessions (remember my car story?), my giving needs to impact my lifestyle in order to get my heart's attention. And when my giving gets my heart's attention, it can get God's attention too.

THE HEART OF WORSHIP

Singing a worship song is not necessarily worship, and neither is writing a check. But when the heart engages in a meaningful way through a praise song or a hymn, it becomes more than just singing. And when the heart engages through a gift that matters, it becomes more than just writing a check.

What about you? Do your gifts engage your heart in worship? Do your gifts influence your lifestyle? Do your gift amounts matter to you?

From God's perspective, *the amount matters.*

Thoughts on Giving

Can you relate to my "two cars" story? What material possession tends to capture your heart?

When was the last time you made a gift decision that moved your heart? What was it about that gift that connected so deeply with your heart?

FOUR

Rule #1:
There Are No Rules

My grandparents were faithful church members. Grandpa served in church leadership, and Grandma sang in the choir. After she passed, I stepped in to help Grandpa with his financial bookkeeping. Each week he gave an amount to the church. At the end of each year, he would ask me to total up the revenue from his various income sources so he could round out his 10 percent tithe.

One day I asked him, "Have you ever thought of giving something different?"

"What do you mean?" he asked.

"Have you ever thought of giving more than 10 percent?"

I shared what I had been learning about giving, adding a few stories from Scripture and my own experience. I could see that something was happening inside him.

With a tear in his eye and a pen in his hand, Grandpa wrote out a check to his church. It was a gift to God and to the place where he had been blessed in so many ways. It was far beyond the amount he gave each month, and even beyond what he typically gave each year. I was familiar with Grandpa's finances, and I was sure of one thing: this was an amount that mattered to him.

For decades he had brought the same gift to the altar each week—one-tenth of his income. I don't think he had ever thought of giving more. His standard for giving, 10 percent off the top, was locked in for life. Almost.

But on that day the ceiling on his gift standard was shattered, and he embraced a significant truth about giving from God's perspective. It's our next Acceptable Gift truth: When it comes to our gifts, *we determine the amount.*

BIBLICAL STANDARDS

There's plenty of debate about whether the Bible insists on a mathematical giving standard. Many suggest the tithe is that standard. Others resist the idea of any biblical giving standard.

Interestingly, there seems to be less urgency to seek a standard for prayer, fasting, Bible study, or church attendance. And how about a metric for honoring your mother and father? It's in the Ten Commandments, but who determines how we live that out?

In His Sermon on the Mount, Jesus provided instructions on giving, praying, and fasting. For each, He focused on the heart standard but did not provide an amount standard (see Matthew 6:1–18). Givers whose stories are told in Scripture include a widow who gave all she had; a repentant tax collector (Zacchaeus) who gave half of his possessions; and the Pharisees, who gave one-tenth of their increase.

How about a clear guideline for acceptable (remember, that would be *pleasing*) praise, prayer, and fasting?

David praised God seven times a day. Daniel prayed to God three times a day. Moses fasted from food and water twice, for forty days straight. Daniel fasted twenty-one days from rich foods and wine. Where did these faith heroes get their standards?

They determined them.

It's human nature to seek something that is concrete, an inviolable guideline, clear marching orders. In other words, *just tell me what to do!*

"What good thing must I do to get eternal life?" the rich young man asked Jesus (Matthew 19:16; Mark 10:17).

"How many times shall I forgive my brother?" asked Peter (Matthew 18:21). These guys are a lot like us.

But let's be honest. Are we looking for a rule to follow so we can check it off the list? Or does a strict rule help to soothe a sense of guilt and confusion? It's always easier to follow rules than to follow a living God.

The absence of rules can cause tension in determining the amount of our gifts. Shouldn't there at least be a minimum? If not, suddenly it's wide open. Multiple options appear. Abel likely dealt with this tension and chose his gift from the firstborn of his flock. Zacchaeus may have encountered this tension concerning his decision—ultimately—to give half of his possessions to the poor. God does not ease this struggle with a one-size-fits-all gift standard. This tension is healthy, and it exists because of our free will. This tension exists because God is not an IRS form; He is our Father who wants a relationship with us.

Think about a meaningful gift you have given to someone you treasure most—perhaps it was a birthday gift, an anniversary gift, or a graduation gift. Who determined the amount of these gifts? You did, right? The giver determines the gift. The same goes for gifts to God.

The problem with my grandfather's giving was not that he followed a giving standard. Standards are powerful tools that help us lock in healthy giving disciplines. Stephanie and I set personal giving standards, and we help our children set them too. Everyone should determine a personal giving standard in their budget.

And the problem wasn't the 10 percent standard. The tithe served me well early in my journey. It is a solid amount for new givers and likely was for Grandpa early in his faith walk.

The problem with Grandpa's standard was that it was never really *his*. He saw it as the church's standard, the denomination's standard, and even God's standard. He was just a few years from his death before realizing the power and control he had over his gift decisions.

God is not looking for the same gift from all His children. He wants a personal gift.

A striped tie for Dad on Father's Day can surely bring him joy. But the exact same tie year after year can lose its appeal. And if we give it because we think that's what he's expecting, the gift is even less personal.

Don't let your gifts to God be like the Father's Day tie. Remember, when we give we should be looking up to God—not down.

FREEWILL GIVING IS NOT NEW

Years ago I learned of a church congregation that decided to no longer teach tithing as a giving principle.

They replaced the tithe language with terms such as *free-will giving* and *grace giving*. Their explanation was that the 10 percent rule was the Old Testament giving standard and no longer applied. New Covenant giving, they concluded, is governed by grace, not law.

I cringed when I heard this. It wasn't their position on tithing that stirred me up (a topic we'll look at later). It was their position on freewill giving as a new concept. Our freewill choice is as old as humanity. And freewill giving was the bedrock of the Old Testament giving system.

Most people think that those living under the Old Covenant had everything spelled out for them. They just had rules to follow, like automatic tax withholding from a paycheck, right?

Nope.

Under the Mosaic Law, God commanded the people to bring gifts to Him at the three annual festivals. "No one should appear before the LORD empty-handed" (Deuteronomy 16:16). But it was each person's responsibility to determine the overall amount "according to the blessings given to them by the LORD" (Deuteronomy 16:17, NLT).

There were eight gift categories under the Law. For half of these, the amount was determined by the giver. For the others, it was determined by the Law. What most people today call "New Testament giving" or "freewill giving" was in full force under the Law. (See chart on page 51. For more research, visit AcceptableGift.org.)

What was particularly delightful about the Plastic Donut exchange with my daughter, Autumn, was that I was not expecting it. It came from her own free will. There is something about unsolicited gifts, determined by the giver, that makes them far more pleasing to the recipient. It's the very essence of giving!

FREEWILL COMMANDS—A PARADOX

Just because God gives us the freedom to determine our gifts, that does not mean any random choice is a pleasing one to Him. To choose not to give freely and willingly is to ignore God's clear desires. This sounds paradoxical, doesn't it? How can we be commanded to

Category	Who Determined the Amount?	Burnt Animals	Non-Burnt Grain	Non-Burnt Animals	Land, Money, Other
Burnt, Peace Offerings	Giver	✓			
Sin, Guilt Offerings	Law	✓			
Vows, Freewill Gifts	Giver	✓	✓	✓	✓
Firstborn Gifts	Law	✓		✓	
Firstfruits	Giver		✓		
Temple Tax	Law				✓
Gifts to the Poor	Giver		✓	✓	✓
Tithes	Law		✓	✓	

do something willingly? Is this a trick? As we'll learn together, we may be free to determine the gift, but it really matters which gift we choose.

God commands us to give freely. These giving instructions come through promptings of the heart. Some of these heart prompts—called direct prompts—are firm and clear. Some are less so, like whispers from God.

Direct Prompts

If anyone is poor among your fellow Israelites…
be openhanded and freely lend them whatever
they need.… There will always be poor people
in the land. Therefore *I command you to be
openhanded* toward your fellow Israelites who
are poor and needy in your land. (Deuteronomy
15:7–8, 11)

Then celebrate the Festival of Weeks to the
LORD your God by giving a freewill offering in
proportion to the blessings the LORD your God
has given you. (Deuteronomy 16:10)

Direct prompts are commands from God that direct our gifts. The Israelites were commanded to give freely and liberally to the poor. They were also instructed to bring freewill gifts to the festival. These commands seemed to carry the weight of the Law.

In both cases, the prompts were firm and clear. Whether to give freewill gifts to the poor or at the festival was not an option. However, the givers used their free choice to determine the amount of the gift. Scriptures are filled with direct-prompt commands such as these.

Direct prompts from God may also be triggered in other ways: during prayer, through conversations with others, while enjoying a concert or a baseball game, or while watching a movie with your family. However you receive these prompts, they are your opportunity to obey.

Jesus delivered a prompt directly to the rich young ruler, inviting the man to sell everything he had and give the money to the poor. It was a clear, unmistakable request. Sadly, the young man declined.

Up Close and Personal

Steve and Angie were sitting in church one Sunday when a funding campaign was being launched. A large gift amount flashed through Steve's mind. It was an amount that mattered to him, an amount far greater than any he and Angie had ever given. After church, Angie shared her thoughts about the campaign. Steve was shocked when she shared the same amount he had been thinking of. They knew this was a prompt from the Lord, so they obeyed.

David was attending a conference when a ministry leader asked him to prayerfully consider funding a particular project. David was surprised to receive such a request, especially for such a large amount. He shared the request with his wife and she was surprised as well. This was undoubtedly an amount that mattered to them.

Shortly afterward they learned of unexpected revenue they would soon receive. The amount and the timing matched up with the need they had been asked to pray about. They knew God was speaking to them, so they obeyed and committed the gift.

God had sent direct prompts to the hearts of these four givers. The instructions were clear to them. Each was a call for obedience in giving a freewill gift. In both cases, the givers' connection to God grew stronger and their faith was strengthened. The gifts far exceeded their usual giving standards and produced a surprising sense of adventure and joy.

Whispers

Tell the Israelites to bring me an offering. You are to receive the offering for me from everyone whose heart prompts them to give. (Exodus 25:2)

Like direct prompts, whisper prompts help us act on the command to give freewill gifts. But unlike direct prompts that are loud and clear, whispers are subtle nudges from God. On one hand, God "commanded" the Israelites to give toward the tabernacle construction (see Exodus 35:4). Surely everyone knew about the materials that were needed. On the other hand, God directed Moses to collect gifts specifically from those whose hearts were prompted. It seemed to be a soft appeal, not a firm one. In the end, freewill offerings were received from those "who were willing" (Exodus 35:29).

While direct prompts often occur unexpectedly (that's why they are more obvious), whisper prompts often are heard when God's children are looking for them. As the gift-giving journey progresses, a person hears the whispers more frequently. God used direct-prompt commands to draw Stephanie and me out of our giving comfort zone. As we obeyed the prompts, we experienced new joys in giving and connected with God in fresh ways. Suddenly we found ourselves looking for further giving experiences. What we once considered comfort-zone threats became appealing giving opportunities. And we began to recognize the whisper prompts more regularly.

PROMPTS ARE
LIKE SNOWFLAKES

Cringe alerts can sound when the topics of freewill gifts and commands are combined in the same sentence. It screams contradiction, or maybe split personality. This is partly because giving prompts—whether the direct kind or the more subtle whispers—are like snowflakes. No two are exactly alike. Not everyone experiences them the same way.

I once experienced a heart prompt while listening to a man share his story about giving. Meanwhile, a friend who heard the same testimony found it to be offensive. His heart was not prompted at all.

On another occasion, I was listening to a giving message at a banquet. The message did nothing for me, but it generated heart prompts for other people seated at my table.

Sometimes heart prompts strike us uniquely at different times. Have you ever read a familiar Scripture passage, but this time the words jumped off the page in ways they had not done before? The command may not have been new to you. But this time it penetrated your heart differently, calling for obedience and action.

Or maybe you see a needy person on the street differently than how you've seen the needy in the past. It might even be the same person you've seen before, but for some reason this time you feel something different inside.

God initiates heart prompts to draw you near to Him. He knows what a particular giving opportunity will do for you and what it can do for Him too. When you notice a prompt in your heart, you should take it personally because it *is* personal.

HEART PROMPTS CAN FADE

So I thought it necessary to urge the brothers to
visit you in advance and finish the arrangements
for the generous gift you had promised. Then
it will be ready as a generous gift, not as one
grudgingly given. (2 Corinthians 9:5)

One of the sobering truths about heart prompts is that they can fade. Years ago a good friend was going through a deep valley. He was broke financially and facing serious legal challenges, and his family had deserted him. He was a dear friend, a "brother in need." God prompted my heart with the following:

If anyone has material possessions and sees a
brother or sister in need but has no pity on
them, how can the love of God be in that
person? Dear children, let us not love with
words or speech but with actions and in truth.
(1 John 3:17–18)

Stephanie and I talked about helping my friend. We
even discussed a specific amount from our savings that
we might give. But I delayed. Eventually the prompt
faded and we never gave the gift.

Paul found the Christians living in Corinth to be in
a similar situation. They had promised to make a freewill gift for those in need. But like me, the believers in
Corinth were slow on the follow-through. They delayed,
then delayed some more. The initial prompts were
fading.

Paul stepped in with some strong encouragement.
In our Bible it's a two-chapter nudge note, known as
2 Corinthians 8–9. It is loaded with prompts. Paul
wanted their gift to be a generous one—an amount that
mattered to them. And he wanted them to stop putting

things off. So he set up processes to help them follow through.

Paul did everything he could to help these folks give an acceptable gift. And he did not provide them an amount to give. He knew that was theirs to determine. He told them, "Each of you should give *what you have decided* in your heart to give, not reluctantly or under compulsion, for God loves a cheerful giver" (2 Corinthians 9:7).

I have always regretted not acting on my earlier prompt. By God's grace, my friend has recovered, but I still feel a twinge when I remember the opportunity to bless that faded.

FREEDOM AND RESPONSIBILITY

The bottom line is this: *we determine the amount* of our gifts. There is tremendous God-given freedom in that—and responsibility too. As you take greater ownership of a relationship with your Father, you may be sensing that you have more responsibility.

Giving is not a touchy-feely thing. You do not give

only when you feel like it or wait until you're prompted. Action is involved and personal standards should be set. Remember, *the amount matters*.

As you move forward in relationship with God, you'll find these two forces, freedom and responsibility, working together in a very natural, freeing way.

▬ ▬ ▬ ▬ ▬ ▬ Thoughts on Giving

How have certain giving rules been helpful to you? How have they been obstacles?
Have you experienced heart promptings from God? What action(s) did the promptings lead to?

FIVE

A Two Percent Perspective

I f Scripture makes it clear that we are to determine the
amount of our gifts, why does the tithe amount keep
popping into our minds? (Yeah, mine too!) I'll tell you
why; it's because we can't escape it. Tithing is the domi-
nant theme used to express views on biblical giving—
and the questions too.

Since this is a short giving book (I mentioned that,
right?), we must stay focused. That's why this message
will not unpack the tithes of Abraham, Jacob, Malachi,
Melchizedek, or the Pharisees. Nor is *Plastic Donuts* a
message about triggering blessings, dodging curses, sowing seeds, or not robbing God.

You also won't hear any ideas about how the tithe was for farmers, not fishermen; was applied to crops, not currency; was actually the last tenth, not the first; was expected to be given two or three times annually, not just once.

But you *will* hear more about this: *acceptable gifts*. Remember, that's our theme. As with all of the Donut approach to giving, it's necessary to step aside from the crowd and go against the grain to see truths that have been obscured by generations of ingrained tradition. Since the crowds are dense on both sides of the tithe debate, a fresh perspective is in order.

FULL PERSPECTIVE

If you've spent any time studying giving statistics, you likely know about the 2 percent. That's the percentage of income people give, on average, to charitable or religious causes. I agree it's a disappointing stat—not the measurement, but what it means. It falls well short of the 10 percent standard that has been held up as a minimum level for biblical giving.

But there is a different 2 percent statistic that is more alarming to me, and it might help explain the first statistic. Of nearly two thousand mentions of various gifts in the Bible (I know because I've counted them), just over forty pertain to the tithe!

That means that mentions of tithing account for only 2 percent of the total gift references in the Bible. So in essence, a tithe-only focus ignores 98 percent of God's guidance on giving. Perhaps today's 2 percent giving is the result of working with an incomplete giving doctrine.

When we don't consider the wholeness of God's Word on a subject, such as giving, things get messy. And because of this disconnect, the matter of the biblical tithe has split the crowd.

SPLIT DECISION

A recent survey of the one-hundred-member board of the National Association of Evangelicals showed that 58 percent do not believe the Bible *requires* tithing, while 42 percent believe it does.

"Required for what?" you ask. Good question. Required for salvation? Required to be in good standing with God? Required to be a good Christian?

The survey is not clear, but it really doesn't matter. When I see surveys such as this one, no matter how the question is worded, the responses are usually divided along similar lines.

For those who are wondering what the fuss is all about, the tithe means "one-tenth." The practice of giving tenths to God traces its origin to the Old Testament. Today tithing for Christians looks like giving 10 percent of one's income to the church. However, not everyone agrees about the treatment of an old giving rule under a new grace covenant. That's why folks want to know, "What are the rules for tithing today?"

When I speak to groups about giving, there is a consistent set of questions people ask. Most pertain to tithing.

- Does the tithe still apply today?
- Should we tithe on the gross or the net?
- Must the tithe go to the church?

- Can we give of our time as part of our tithe?
- Should we tithe on inheritances? insurance settlements? the profit realized from selling a home? tax refunds? plastic toys? (Okay, I made that last one up!)

People want to know what the Bible says. I understand. I had the same questions.

But as we continue to look at giving, we can find sound answers to the most frequently asked tithing questions. The answers are found in the Acceptable Gift truths. We have seen two of them so far, and there are two more to come. So hang in there with me.

WHAT DID JESUS SAY?

If anyone had a chance to clear the air on tithing, it would be Jesus. But He didn't do so. He did make two statements (yeah, that's all) about the tithe that are recorded in Scripture (see Matthew 23:23; Luke 18:11–14). In both accounts He rebukes a tithe-abiding Pharisee for the condition of his heart. Desperate to find a silver-bullet passage to settle the debate, Bible teachers are divided in their interpretations of what, exactly, Jesus meant in His references to the tithe.

When He spoke to the disciples about giving, Jesus did not bring up the tithe. Instead, He said, "Give, and it will be given to you.... For with the measure you use, it will be measured to you" (Luke 6:38).

When He spoke to the crowds, He said, "Store up for yourselves treasures in heaven" (Matthew 6:20).

When the Pharisees asked Jesus about paying the Caesar tax, He responded, "So give back to Caesar what is Caesar's, and to God what is God's" (Matthew 22:21).

These are not statements that provide clear guidance on tithing. Perhaps this was purposeful. When it comes to questions such as, "What measure should I use?" or "How much treasure should I store up?" and "How much is God's?" the timeless principles apply. They are: *the amount matters,* and *we determine the amount.*

The apostle Paul also had a chance to clear the air on tithing, but he didn't. As the writer of nearly half of the New Testament books, Paul said much about giving, but he did not make a direct connection to how the tithe applies today. Neither did Peter, James, or John.

As for this lack of New Testament guidance on tithing, some teachers say this proves the tithe was not the New Covenant standard. Others claim this tradition was so firmly embedded in practice that it needed no mention by Jesus or the disciples. See what I mean?

CHURCH GIVING—IT'S CLEAR

While the case for the tithe may not be clear to everyone, the case for church giving should be. The matter of church giving is not exclusively tied to the tithe. Regardless of what one believes about tithing today, our responsibility to support the church is well grounded in the Scriptures.

When Jesus commissioned the first preachers for their travel assignments, He told them not to take any money or possessions. He instructed them instead to search for "some worthy person" who would support their needs (Matthew 10:9–11). Even before His death and resurrection, the funding precedent for supporting the church had been set by Jesus.

The apostle Paul used direct prompts to command us to share materially with those who feed us spiritually (see 1 Corinthians 9:9–14). This includes gifts to support preachers, teachers, and directors of church affairs (see 1 Timothy 5:17–18). Like Jesus, Paul was clear about supporting the ministries and leaders of the church.

MIXED SIGNALS?

You may have mixed reactions to this chapter. I expect that. You may feel unsettled by the idea that the tithe standard is not so clear. Or you could sense a new freedom about *determining* the matter of the tithe for yourself. That's good. But remember, there is responsibility too. *The amount matters.*

We can all agree on this much: personal standards are helpful, and encouraged. Still, more clarity is needed. How do we determine our personal giving levels—the amount to give to God? Is there another standard that might help us?

That's what the next chapter is about.

▬ ▬ ▬ ▬ ▬ ▬ Thoughts on Giving

Why do you think the tithing issue has generated so much confusion?

How does the discussion in this chapter make you feel?

SIX

Because You Can

Have you heard expressions like these?

"If church members would give at least 10 percent of their incomes, an additional $164 billion would be available to finance kingdom work every year."

"If ten million people chose to give just twenty dollars a week—equal to the cost of five trips to Starbucks—a staggering amount, $10.4 billion, would be available to advance God's kingdom."

Or how about the Giving Pledge? Bill and Melinda Gates and Warren Buffett have called the world's wealthiest people to pledge more than half their wealth to charities during their lifetime or after their death.

I commend such good-hearted expressions. I would like to see all Christians giving at least 10 percent of their incomes. And I would like to see the world's wealthy give half their possessions to the poor, as Zacchaeus did. And while such funding equations might seem to resolve the world's inequities, God does not express His economy in these ways.

God has a different financial model for solving the world's inequities. It's captured in the next truth about giving acceptable gifts: God desires everyone to *give according to their abilities.* It's a simple plan.

ABILITY GIVING—AN ACCEPTABLE STANDARD

> The gift is acceptable *according to what one has,* not according to what one does not have.
> (2 Corinthians 8:12)

Before he was renamed Paul, Saul was the strictest of Pharisees, following all the known religious rules. Whatever commitment to tithing he once held, we have no record of his giving further instruction about it.

But he was clear about one giving standard—the ability standard.

As the needs of famine-stricken Judeans morphed to crisis levels, Paul asked the believers living in Corinth to give a special kind of gift, an acceptable gift. That is a gift that is based on the giver's means (see 2 Corinthians 8:11). In other words, the gift is based on the person's abilities.

The Macedonians are mentioned in Scripture for giving generously, and without needing to be reminded. Paul mentioned further that they gave "according to their *ability,* and beyond..." (2 Corinthians 8:3, NASB). He wanted the believers in Corinth to apply the same standard.

You may wonder how Paul came up with the ability standard. Consider three sources:

Ability Giving—a Christian Standard

So for a whole year Barnabas and Saul met with the church and taught great numbers of people. The disciples were called Christians first at Antioch. (Acts 11:26)

After being devoted to persecuting Christ followers, Saul had a conversion experience. During a boot camp training season, he witnessed one of the most striking characteristics of a group given the name "Christians." A prophet named Agabus prophesied that a severe famine would cover the Roman Empire. That must have been a prompt to these "little Christs." Notice how they acted in response:

> So the disciples *determined,* every one according
> to his *ability,* to send relief to the brothers living
> in Judea. And they did so, sending it to the
> elders by the hand of Barnabas and Saul. (Acts
> 11:29–30, esv)

It had not been long since Saul had presided over the ugly, brutal persecution of Christ followers. (Remember Stephen?) Now this same man was presiding over receiving acceptable gifts to the poor—gifts from the very Christians he once set out to kill. Wow!

Ability is not a new idea. Based on the earliest biblical definitions, Christians are those who give according to their abilities.

Ability Giving—Christ's Standard

> Truly I tell you, this poor widow has put more into the treasury than all the others. They all gave out of their wealth; but she, out of her poverty, put in everything—all she had to live on. (Jesus, in Mark 12:43–44)

I'm sure Paul heard about the account of the widow who gave "two very small copper coins," worth a fraction of a penny (Mark 12:42). Jesus contrasted her gift with the giving of the rich. Even though she was poor, the widow had a benchmark for a superior gift—it was her ability.

In addition, the story about the prosperous but foolish farmer would have influenced Paul's convictions about giving. Jesus rebuked the farmer because he stored up his wealth for himself but was "not rich toward God" (Luke 12:21).

Jesus did not say the farmer was not a giver. He may even have been a tither. All we know is that he was not rich toward God. The "rich toward God" standard is connected to our ability.

Ability Giving—an Old Testament Standard

Paul, being an expert in the Jewish Law, would have been aware of the ability standard from the Old Testament. God has been measuring gifts based on the giver's ability for a long time. Here is how we know this:

A capital campaign was launched to finance construction of the tabernacle building. The Israelites were told, *"From what you have,* take an offering for the LORD" (Exodus 35:5).

David understood the ability standard. He told God, "Now with all my *ability* I have provided for the house of my God the gold…silver…bronze…iron… wood…onyx stones…" (1 Chronicles 29:2, NASB).

As part of the temple rebuilding campaign years later, the people gave freewill offerings to the temple treasury "according to their ability" (see Ezra 2:69).

And beyond gifts given in response to a specific need, there were the three annual festivals. For each, the people were commanded: "No one should appear before the LORD empty-handed: Each of you must bring a gift in proportion to the way the LORD your God has blessed you" (Deuteronomy 16:16–17).

In the case of the burnt offering, each person was to offer this voluntary gift according to his possessions. If he owned a herd, then he would offer a bull. If he did not have cattle but had sheep or goats instead, then the burnt offering came from the flock. If the Israelite did not have a herd or a flock, the offering could be a turtledove or a pigeon. The acceptable gift was determined on the basis of the giver's means, or ability.

A Pigeon for a Lamb

After Jesus was born, Mary took Him to the temple to be consecrated to the Lord. She offered a sacrifice in keeping with the Law: "a pair of doves or two young pigeons" (Luke 2:24). This suggests Mary could not afford a lamb. According to the Law, she could offer two birds—one as a sin offering for the ceremonial purification and the other as a voluntary burnt offering in place of a lamb (see Leviticus 12:8). Mary gave gifts based on her ability.

It is ironic that to a mother who had no lamb to give, God would give His Lamb instead. She would raise God's Son and love Him as her very own. Thirty-three years later this Lamb would give of His complete ability, His life and blood, as the acceptable gift for the sins of the world.

This Lamb was a gift to God and a gift for us. When we give according to our ability, we honor the One who gave all of His ability.

ABILITY GIVING TODAY

After Stephanie and I married and merged our finances, we began to give jointly. The only giving standard either of us had observed prior to being married was the tithe. But after the Sunday school experience I shared earlier, we began to ask the famous question: "Should we give 10 percent of our gross income or net income?"

When you approach such a question with an open

heart, God's promptings begin to work. This process is not without some tension. For us, the decision to give more would involve trade-offs, meaning less of our income would be available for things we really enjoyed. These things involved amounts that mattered to us. But we couldn't ignore God's promptings. As we started to look up, rather than down, with our gifts, we wanted the amount of each gift to matter too. Ultimately, we determined to give the greater amount for one simple reason: because we could. We had the ability.

Then new questions surfaced. Are we to give just 10 percent? Should we give 11 percent, or even 20? What is the biblical standard? I continued to flip through my Bible, looking for the most direct, most applicable rules on giving. I didn't find the chapter that had the rules, but we did discover plenty of prompts.

Like before, these decisions involved trade-offs. But the more we considered the prompts, the more clearly we saw God's blessings in our lives—salvation, family, peace, contentment, provision. Somehow this perspective caused us to view our ability to give more plainly, while our limitations began to fade into the background.

Instead of asking why give more, we began to ask why not? Giving decisions became easier.

With each step in the journey came a deeper connection with God. Sometimes we experienced His touch through direct financial blessings. At other times we didn't notice anything material—but rather a peace that surpasses all understanding. It was a smile from God as He took pleasure in our gifts.

PROFIT, POSSESSION, AND PAID-FOR ABILITIES

A friend of mine made a commitment to give as part of a church capital campaign. His three-year pledge was based on an anticipated revenue source. Three years later, the expected revenue had not been received. In a sense, my friend felt he was released from his pledge... but not completely.

After prayer, reflection, and sensitivity to prompts, he recognized he could still give the gift based on his possession (asset) ability. His boat, a prized possession, was worth the amount of his giving commitment. So he sold the boat and gave his gift to God. My friend discovered the truth of giving more because you can. He had the ability, and he gave accordingly.

His gift also represented the heart shift we've seen in so many people: instead of finding reasons *not* to give, he looked for ways to be a joyful giver.

There is another ability we may have. I call it "paid-for" ability. Suppose your son or daughter receives a college scholarship. The money you may have set aside to help cover the cost of tuition is now available to you again, increasing your ability to give. Or maybe your employer has provided you with a company car or car allowance. This stretches your personal budget dollars, increasing your giving ability. Maybe your employer provides your cell phone. Again, this increases your ability. Maybe a friend unexpectedly buys your lunch. You now have an unexpected ability to give.

You may not think you have the ability to give. But if you pay attention, you'll be surprised at just what abilities you really do have.

LIFESTYLE CHOICES

Tapping your true giving ability will require countercultural lifestyle choices—such as debt-free living or a reduction in your spending. Unfortunately, many of us have already forfeited our giving ability due to poor financial choices. Just a few unplanned moves can tie up your giving ability. For many, debt is a big one. Or maybe it's not debt, but rather lifestyle indulgences that drain money every month out of your available income or assets. The good news is that a few planned moves can also free up your ability to give.

Years ago Stephanie and I made the commitment to become completely debt-free so we could direct the savings toward our giving lifestyle. We made sacrifices to reach our goals. Once we paid off our home, we were able to commit more of our ability toward gifts to God. And it's not just us. We have attended the celebrations held by families that have reached debt-free milestones. Instead of using their new freedom to renew efforts to upgrade their lifestyle, they are tapping their regained abilities for gifts to God. We also know families that have downsized in order to restore giving ability to their financial lives.

FAITH ABILITIES

When you have a relationship with the living God, heart prompts will test your faith abilities, not just the financial ones. God may initiate heart prompts to give an amount that matters in a big way. You might not think you can afford the gift. Or maybe you can afford it, but you're not sure how it will affect your retirement, next summer's vacation, or maybe even paying next month's utility bill.

The impoverished Macedonian Christians did not have much financial ability to give. But their faith ability carried them through in giving a powerful gift to the famine-ravaged Judeans. We learn in Hebrews that "without faith it is impossible to please God" (Hebrews 11:6). Since acceptable gifts are gifts that please God, it's reasonable to assume that our giving should involve faith.

Remember, giving is part of our relationship with

God. It is not a duty or a financial formula. As we engage in that relationship through giving, God grows our faith to deepen our walk with Him.

Count Your Blessings

If you want to grow your faith, grow your gratitude. To grow your gratitude, take time to count your blessings.

When you take time to stop and look around you—to look at the people who invest in you and those from the past who helped build your character and your life—you remember things that you can never take credit for. They were given to you, like Grandma's prayers that accompanied you on your salvation journey, like the providence of God that led you to meet your spouse, like the miracle birth of your child, circumstances that allowed you to go to college, the friend of a friend who paved the path for your first job. Once you start counting blessings—many of them ones you have never before acknowledged—you will be overwhelmed. Once you start the list, you'll find it's hard to stop. As you fix your attention on the blessings you have, you'll think less about what you do not have.

I call this tapping your providential abilities. As you recognize the providence of God, your heart will fill with gratitude...and your faith muscles will be strengthened.

OKAY, BACK TO TITHING

When heart prompts sound off, financial abilities start talking and faith abilities begin stretching. All of this helps the giving decisions start to flow. Next thing you know, the detail questions about percentages, Old Covenant rules versus New Covenant rules, and pretax or posttax issues go away. And the peripheral matters of whether to tithe from a tax refund, birthday gift, house sale, or inheritance may lead to entirely new ideas about whether to give a third or a half or even all of it as a gift to God.

You still may not be able to articulate a theological position on the biblical tithe and how it should apply in every situation. But it won't matter. You will find your gifts being guided by ability and the satisfaction of giving acceptable gifts.

But what if you can't? Perhaps you're in a rotten financial situation. You're looking at the piles of bills stacked on your desk and the pink slip from your former employer, and there is no way you can give. The reasons are many: a burdensome debt load, a marriage crisis, an extended period of unemployment, a medical crisis, or all of the above.

The story of the New Testament widow shows that most of us always have something to give. Elijah instructed a widow to give her very last meal. Even as she and her son were about to die of hunger, she learned she still had an ability to give (see 1 Kings 17:10–16). In that instance, God worked an ongoing miracle. It's worth reading the story.

There may be times when you need to take ownership of your past financial decisions and the damaging consequences and seek forgiveness. You might have to make some gut-wrenching decisions, such as selling your home, forgoing a vacation, taking your child out of private school, or canceling satellite television. I have a friend who went a full year without eating out—even cheap, fast food—so he could reduce his debt.

As you take these steps, making room for gifts to God, He will notice. You might not be able to give much, and your faith ability might be running low. But rest assured that your gift can still reach God. No matter what your ability or inability, God can be pleased with your gift.

COMING TO PEACE
WITH THE TENSIONS

I don't believe the questions ever go away completely. And even if we could put behind us all the questions that came up already, there would be new ones. Giving is not cut-and-dried, which is why discussion and investigation are important. How simply should I live? How much debt is too much? How much home is too much? Is going on a cruise too extravagant? How much savings do I really need? If you experience these tensions, that's good. I have them too.

But by now, we have clear scriptural guidelines that address these types of questions. When it comes to our gifts, we know *the amount matters*. And when selecting our gifts, *we determine the amount,* in order to delight our Father.

In measuring whether our gift is the acceptable kind, God measures it *according to our ability.* He understands our ability and takes it into consideration, not as a celestial bill collector, but as a loving Father.

There always will be a healthy tension within us as we live the Christian life. At the same time, there is a growing peace deep within that comes through a connection to God—a connection that deepens with giving acceptable gifts to Him.

Thoughts on Giving

What giving abilities that you were previously unaware of have come to light?

Which types of abilities do you want to exercise more in your giving?

SEVEN

All the Difference

The sanctuary was at full capacity on Harvest Sunday. It was the final day for celebrating the capital campaign and for everyone to bring their gifts to the altar.

Chuck stood with his wife, Ellen, in the row directly behind the pastor. Ellen noticed that Chuck was restless throughout the service, but she didn't think anything of it. As the campaign chairman, Chuck had extended several public appeals to the congregation. He and Ellen also had conducted a series of vision-casting sessions in homes.

They were emotionally invested in the campaign

and had committed a significant personal gift. At the appropriate time, the pastor stepped up to the pulpit to invite members of the congregation to bring their gifts. After a heartfelt prayer, the music began and Chuck stepped into the aisle with Ellen. He knew his quick action would serve as a cue for the rest of the congregation to follow.

Ellen and Chuck knelt at the altar for prayer. A crowd began to surround them at the platform. Chuck and Ellen stood up and walked past the decorated treasure chest. Chuck dropped an envelope into the box. As they returned to their seats, Chuck's palms were sweaty. With one arm behind Ellen, hugging her waist, he clenched his other fist inside his pocket. And inside the fist was the check.

Ellen did not know that the envelope they dropped in the treasure chest was empty.

When the service was over, Chuck gathered his family and left as quickly as he could. After a hurried lunch at home, he went to his office. (He had told Ellen he had something to take care of.)

Sitting at his desk, he struggled with what he had to do. He finally pulled out his phone and made the call. It was a call he had thought about for years, but a mixture of fear and pride had always stepped in the way.

"James, this is Chuck."

It had been a few years since the men had seen each other. It had been even longer since they had talked cordially, without attorneys in the room. Despite the lapse in time, no introduction was necessary.

"James, I want you to know I really regret what happened. I know there's much water under the bridge and that we failed to resolve things out of court. I am truly sorry for my part in it all. I hope you will forgive me."

The conversation was short.

Chuck knew they would never be best friends again. They wouldn't play golf or attend civic events together. Yet something significant took place as a result of the phone call. A burden was lifted from Chuck's heart.

He placed his cell phone on his desk; then he leaned back in his chair and sighed. After a moment of reflection, he stood up to leave and reached into his pocket to feel the check. Of course he knew it was still there. He left the office and called Ellen to explain the situation. On the way home, he stopped by the church and went inside to leave their check.

The gift was now complete—and acceptable.

DON'T LEAVE HOME WITHOUT IT

Therefore, if you are offering your gift at the altar and there remember that your brother or sister has something against you, leave your gift there in front of the altar. First go and be reconciled to them; then come and offer your gift. (Jesus, in Matthew 5:23–24)

May I ask you to read Jesus's giving instructions again? It's important. What would you say He is more concerned about: the money, or something else?

We often hear, "It's all about the heart." But do we know what that means? When my dad first taught me about communion, I realized it was my chance to clear my conscience. It was a way of seeing the priority God places on the condition of my heart as I seek to engage with Him.

Ananias and Sapphira learned this heart lesson the hard way. They gave a special gift but lacked the proper heart to go with it. They lied to God about their gift. What started as a freewill gift expression ended with a tragic family funeral (see Acts 5:1–10).

When it comes to our gifts, we know already that *the amount matters.* We know as well that *we determine the amount,* and we know God measures the gift *based on our ability.* These are marks of an acceptable gift.

But we learn one more truth about giving an acceptable gift. In the end, it is *the condition of the giver's heart* that makes the gift pleasing to God.

THE HEART VERSUS THE GIFT

To do what is right and just is *more acceptable* to the LORD than sacrifice. (Proverbs 21:3)

Does the LORD delight in burnt offerings and sacrifices as much as in obeying the LORD? To

obey is better than sacrifice, and to heed is better
than the fat of rams. (1 Samuel 15:22)

God desired the hearts of the Israelites over the
blood of animals. And today He desires the hearts of His
children over their gifts of money and possessions. Even
Jesus acknowledged that it wasn't His body that God
desired; it was His submission to God's will (see Hebrews 10:5–7).

Remember, our money is like the gift of Plastic Donuts to Him. And this is where it gets tricky. On one
hand, God doesn't want our gifts without our hearts
being clear. On the other hand, we have seen that without gifts, our hearts cannot fully express love for God or
others.

Just because more than one thing is desired—and
one is more highly sought than the other—does not
mean that the other is not desired. Make sense? Without a heart that pleases God, our gifts have limited
value. And without gifts that please God, our heart expression is limited.

NOT ONE OR THE OTHER

I'd prefer my little girl's heart over a Plastic Donut any day. But I sure enjoy having both. And how could I see that I had my little girl's heart if it weren't for her actions? That is the case with God, and it helps explain why He designed us this way.

As we learned earlier, our hearts and our stuff are connected. That means that a primary way we speak from our hearts is through our gifts. Paul instructed the Corinthians to prove their love by their gifts (see 2 Corinthians 8:8, 24). James wrote that religion that God accepts as being pure is to look after widows and orphans (see James 1:27). John added that to not share your material possessions with those in need is to not have the love of God in your heart (see 1 John 3:17).

On the flip side, Paul warned the Corinthians that even if a person gives all they have to the poor—but does it without love—the gift is worthless (see 1 Corinthians 13:3). And while the Pharisees were proud of their faithful tithing record, Jesus rebuked them for neglecting "the more important matters of the law—justice, mercy and faithfulness" (Matthew 23:23). He did not let them off the hook for being scrupulous givers. Instead, He admonished them to get their hearts right while continuing their giving.

The gift helps your heart speak what it really feels. And the heart makes your gift count for what it's really worth. The gift and the heart—they work together.

CHRISTIAN PHILANTHROPY

Could it be that a giving lifestyle apart from love and obedience to God is simply philanthropy? Jesus said, "No branch can bear fruit by itself" (John 15:4). A giver who does his work apart from the vine—Jesus—is "like a branch that is thrown away and withers" (John 15:6). Those are hard words, and they say much about the connection of your heart and your gift.

If in the past you operated as a "Christian philanthropist," perhaps now you are beginning to see how giving with a realigned heart can deepen your walk with God. You can relate to the Father in a new way.

GIVE TO GET

Whoever sows sparingly will also reap sparingly,
and whoever sows generously will also reap
generously. (2 Corinthians 9:6)

When it comes to the matter of giving and the
heart, people like to talk about motives. Perhaps the motive that attracts the most chatter is the principle of sowing and reaping. People have strong opinions about that
one on both sides of the issue. For some, sowing and
reaping is a primary motive for giving. Others consider
this to be an inferior motive, the bottom rung on the
ladder of spiritual maturity.

So how does God view sowing and reaping as a
giving motivation?

The "Give to Get" Principle Works
for Papa

My father loves his eight grandchildren, and he knows
his grandchildren love sweets. When he comes out with
a package of cookies or a box of popsicles, the little ones

head in his direction. They crawl to his ankles, up into his lap, saying, "Papa, Papa."

He knows he is appealing to their desires, but he's okay with that. He understands the mind of a child. In fact, if you ask the younger ones why they like going to Papa's house, they might say, "He gives us treats." He likes the attention, and the kids like the sweets. In the process, the rewarding techniques draw the grandchildren closer to Papa—into his arms, his love, and his presence. With time, the attraction to Papa will mature beyond the simple desire for treats.

The children begin to learn his voice, his laugh, his love, his character, and the comfort and security they find in his presence. Their love for Papa becomes more pure. You can see it now in their eyes and when they hug his neck. You can hear it in their voices when they say, "I love you, Papa."

We are God's children, and we should take pleasure in God's rewarding ways, not reject or debate them. If one of the grandchildren would reject Papa's reward, it would dampen his spirit. God wants to reward His children for behavior that pleases Him—behavior that leads toward a connection to Him with greater peace, joy, security, trust, dependence, gratitude, worship, and love.

Rewarding Motivations—That's God's Job

> There is something else meaningless that occurs on earth: the righteous who get what the wicked deserve, and the wicked who get what the righteous deserve. (Ecclesiastes 8:14)

When it comes to the principle of sowing and reaping, not everything shakes out like we think it should. Solomon found it perplexing that the righteous may suffer while the wicked may prosper. But he understood that God's judgment is not finished until later (see Ecclesiastes 12:14).

Often, when we give we experience financial blessings. Sometimes the blessings may come in less tangible forms or in ways we won't fully experience and recognize until eternity. If rewards were predictable, giving would not involve faith.

When we do reap a miraculous return from heaven,

it is natural to become excited. We'll also recognize that something bigger is happening. God is getting our attention.

Remember when Peter helped drag in a net full of fish in response to his obedience to Jesus (see John 21:6)? More important than the fish, Peter experienced the miracle provision of God. Immediately Peter abandoned the fish, jumped out of the boat, and ran to Jesus. Like Papa with a box of treats, God uses miracle blessings to send us running into His arms.

Another reason God blesses us is so we will continue to give from our increasing abilities: "You will be enriched in every way so that you can be generous on every occasion" (2 Corinthians 9:11).

God is the One who measures our motives. And He manages them too, cycling different motives into our lives to develop us in new ways. We don't need to judge the "right" or "wrong" motives for others. Satan thought he understood the motives behind Job's heart and actions. But of course, God knew Job better. God knows the hearts of His children.

BACK TO THE HEART OF THE MATTER

As the father of four children, I've learned a lot about parenting. One of my discoveries is how enjoyable life is for me when my kids have their hearts lined up right. And how painful it is when they do not. But no matter how far they stray, it's easy for them to get back into my fellowship.

Getting to the point of repentance may be difficult, but that's their part. Receiving my forgiveness is instant. When it happens with my children, the breakthrough is powerful. Immediately we're off to a fresh start, like the prodigal son who drifted from his father. The father welcomed the son's return instantly and completely.

Perhaps you started reading this book because you had questions about giving. But now this chapter on the heart has you thinking of something else. Perhaps your heart condition is standing in the way of giving an acceptable gift. It might be a sin problem. It might be an attitude problem. It might be unconfessed wrongs. It might be a strained relationship.

No matter what it is, you are just a few steps away from a heart reset and fellowship restored with God. You may already be on a giving journey, but now you want it to count in new ways. This is your chance to right your heart with God.

Start by looking up, not at your bank statement or your bills or your problems or your past. Look up. Give your heart and soul to God. Then sense His smile. Sense His pleasure in you. Feel His embrace.

Now imagine Him receiving your gift. Like a Plastic Donut in a daddy's hand, your gift falls to heaven's floor as God picks you up in His arms and assures you that what He *really* desires is your heart...and the Donut is just a tool you use to give your heart to Him.

Get that picture?

— — — — — — **Thoughts on Giving**

What do you think it means for you, personally, to give from your heart?

What are the things that help you get your heart clear before God?

EIGHT

That Chair

In my living room is a big, cream-colored leather chair that belonged to my grandfather. It's where I sit while reading the Bible in the mornings. It's where I sit when I address my family for family time. It's the very chair I sat in when Autumn Joy approached me with the Plastic Donut. It's a great chair.

God has a chair like this. A man named John caught a glimpse of it while he received a unique vision. His vision is known as the Revelation of Jesus Christ. In the vision an angel shared scenes from heaven. Among them was one of the most breathtaking gift accounts ever described, and it took place at "that chair."

In John's vision, someone is sitting on a chair or

throne in heaven, and encircling the throne is a rainbow (see Revelation 4:2–3). (It is interesting how rainbows seem to appear at the scene of gifts given to God. Remember God's response to Noah's gift?)

Surrounding the throne is a host of elders. Each elder is dressed in white, wearing a crown of gold and sitting on a separate chair (see Revelation 4:4). The elders are falling down and casting their crowns before the throne.

These crowns were special Donuts—acceptable gifts for sure. Certainly the gold crowns were *amounts that mattered* to the elders. That is why they gave them.

I suspect the elders each *had determined,* freely and willingly, to give their crowns as a natural response to worship. Group-think behavior has no place when standing before that chair.

The elders gave *according to their abilities*—from the crowns on their heads. Ironically, these crowns were likely the rewards they received for how they had stewarded their previous abilities.

And their *hearts*? Well, check this out. As the elders fell before the throne, they cried out,

You are worthy, our Lord and God, to receive
glory and honor and power, for you created all
things, and by your will were created and have
their being. (Revelation 4:11)

Often, when people refer to this scene before the
throne, they talk as if it is a one-time event. Many assume we all will leave our crowns at the throne and walk
away from them forever—sort of like the final scene of a
play. But a closer reading suggests the gift scenario is
being repeated over and over again (see Revelation 4:9).
Throughout eternity, we will bring gifts to that chair as
we worship the King.

From John's Revelation we are told "the kings of
the earth will bring their splendor into" the gates of the
New Jerusalem, heaven's capital city (Revelation 21:24).
There are twelve pearly gates that allow entry into the
city (see Revelation 21:12, 21). Traffic will be busy for
gift travelers.

This is great encouragement to us. God loves His
children, and He loves to be worshiped by them. In
heaven we will appear before His chair and present our

gifts. Until then, we continue to give gifts from afar, gifts of money and possessions that have been entrusted to us while on earth.

I hope you'll remember my story about the Donut, how our gifts today can still reach the Father, even though we are not yet at His chair in heaven.

Online giving, wireless checks, bank drafts, kiosk gift transactions—all of these gift forms can be acceptable to God. These gifts can get the attention, touch the heart, and tap the delight of our almighty God. Your gifts can travel!

The next time you give a gift, remember the Acceptable Gift truths:

- The amount matters.
- We determine the amount.
- We give according to ability.
- The heart makes the gift count.

So bring your gifts to Him. May they be pleasing and acceptable in His sight. And may your face light up as you imagine the joyful approval of your Father as He receives you in one arm…and your Plastic Donuts in the other.

Thoughts on Giving

How has your view of God as *your Father* been impacted by this book?

Postscript:
Ways to Chew on Plastic Donuts

If you have been challenged and encouraged by the truths found in *Plastic Donuts,* here are ways you can help spread the message.

Share Plastic Donuts *with Your Church*

We have additional resources available that you can share with your church. One simple idea is to use it within your congregation: give this book to each family, use it in small group ministry, or discuss it when your church is having a giving emphasis or annual series on stewardship. Go to our website for additional resources (www.acceptablegift.org).

Give Plastic Donuts *as a Gift to Supporters of Your Nonprofit Ministry*

This is a beautiful way to show appreciation and help your constituents grow in their giving journey. You can go to our website to see video testimonials of people who have experienced giving from this fresh perspective.

Share Plastic Donuts *with Friends and Family*

Purchase a dozen copies of the book to pass along to those in your circle of influence. Help us spread these helpful biblical truths by sharing the message with others.

Check Out Our Research

To learn more about the biblical research supporting the Acceptable Gift truths, go to www.acceptablegift.org to sign up for insights and to access free resources and blogs. Join the discussion!

About Jeff

Since childhood, Jeff Anderson has displayed an unexpected blend of behaviors: he is a cautious risk taker. When he was working as an accountant, Jeff daydreamed about being a professional blackjack player. (Key word: *daydream*.) That explains how, after leaving a big-six accounting firm, he became a stock day trader. For the next five years he spent his days staring at computers, skipping bathroom breaks, and riding the waves of the market.

But he constantly reflected on spiritual matters and how God sees our lives. In 2003, he joined Crown Financial Ministries, eventually serving as vice president of North America Generosity Initiatives. After many years there, he established AcceptableGift.org. Jeff encourages people to expect more in their walk with God, as detailed in his book *Divine Applause*. He's married to

Stephanie and has four children: Austin, Cade, Gunnar, and Autumn.

ABOUT ACCEPTABLE GIFT

When the Israelites offered "acceptable sacrifices," the aroma drifted to the heavens. God noticed. God was pleased. And His children knew it.

Deep down, we all want to know God is pleased with our lives, but can we *really* know? An acceptable gift pleases God, gets His attention, and connects us. Spiritual activities such as giving were created to bring us closer to God! AcceptableGift.org spreads the message of giving from God's perspective and helps people find clarity, freedom, and inspiration to live differently.

Secrets and Rewards of Walking with An Invisible God

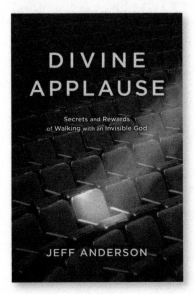

Like any dynamic personal connection, walking with an invisible God requires two-way engagement. There are things we can do and ways to view God differently that can give us the connection we're looking for.

"Attention is something children will cry for and adults will die for. Jeff shows us how we can connect with God's blessing and applause."

—JIM STOVALL, Author & Emmy Award winner, *The Ultimate Gift*

"God's love isn't based on our performance. But He does want us to actively engage with Him, to get His "attention." *Divine Applause* offers practical guidance to make that a deeper reality in our lives."

—JIM DALY, President, Focus on the Family

www.DivineApplause.com

Expect more...
from your journey with God

The Acceptable Gift is not a common message, and Jeff Anderson is out to bring light to this crucial biblical perspective, with a fresh understanding that God notices our lives.

His research and counsel has also helped many church and non-profit leaders.

As a speaker, Jeff challenges people to:

- **See God differently — more personally**
- **Expect more from their journey with God**
- **Step into new experiences with God**

When we see our lives from His perspective, we'll see God differently, and we'll live differently.

For our free newsletter, or to contact us about your needs and schedule, please go to www.AcceptableGift.org

ACCEPTABLE gift
Living & Giving from God's Perspective